SIX WORD LESSONS™

ON

EFFECTIVE COMMUNICATION

100 Lessons
to Show up Well
in Personal and Professional
Communication

Jenni Butz

TheWordSpark.com

Six-Word Lessons on Effective Communication

Published by Pacelli Publishing
9905 Lake Washington Blvd. NE, #D-103
Bellevue, Washington 98004
PacelliPublishing.com

ISBN-10: 1-933750-57-X
ISBN-13: 978-1-933750-57-6

Contents

Acknowledgements

While many of these lessons have been taught by teachers and professors over the years, the most important ones have been learned by trial and error at the expense of those closest to me. Thank you, Tony and Charlie, my grace-filled husband and resilient son, for bearing with my bumbling communication over the years as I learn. You both model the best of communication in your unique ways, and I'm proud to have gleaned from you and am humbled to pass our lessons on to others.

Introduction

Whether in a professional setting or among our most intimate relationships, effective communication can mean the difference between success and failure. Our words express and expose our deepest thoughts and feelings, so it behooves us to be intentional and meticulous. My hope in these lessons is that you will remember your high school English teacher fondly and that you will take to heart any communication lessons you learned in years of therapy or in the wake of broken relationships so that you can speak boldly, respectfully, and effectively in any environment.

Six-Word Lessons on Effective Communication

Proactive Communication Skills: Moving Things Forward

1

Communication's purpose: to understand and influence.

While it's tempting to believe that communication's end goal is to hear our own voices or to regale others with tales of our professional prowess or hilarious antics, the truth is that communication is simply the way we connect with others. Effective communication should move understanding forward and accomplish goals that benefit the population.

2

Being clear and concise communicates well.

Preparation is key in having successful communication, enabling us to use the best words and methods possible to convey crucial points. Reminding ourselves of what we want to talk about and the main goal of important conversations increases the odds of actually staying on topic and of others tracking with us as we speak.

3

Words reflect *and* influence our attitudes.

Because the words we use reveal underlying attitudes, we can look back on unfortunate conversations and realize that what we wanted out of the conversation wasn't at all what we *said* we wanted. However, being intentional to use positive language that reflects the attitude we *want* to have, will allow us to change our attitudes to what we've been talking about.

4

"Can you do what I want?"

Communicate tasks, deadlines and parameters clearly to team members, and don't be afraid to ask specifically for what you want. (With a kind tone, of course!) The benefit of a clear request is that there is less room for passive/aggressive language and behavior when others don't pick up what we think are obvious cues.

5

Examine motives in conversations gone wrong.

When the wheels fall off a conversation and we are wondering where things went wrong, two questions can be helpful in examining our own part in the breakdown. 1) What was I hoping for? 2) Where did that come from? This reveals underlying motives or areas in our lives that need to be addressed to avoid future issues.

6

Consistent good communication equals quality relationships.

Because mutual understanding is the glue that holds personal or professional relationships together, it behooves us to communicate as well as possible as often as possible. Establishing and maintaining new patterns in connecting with others is the most important way to ensure that those relationships are healthy and productive when they need to be.

7

Assess surroundings before having major conversations.

Significant conversations need quiet, uninterrupted time, and space away from listening ears and those who would participate without being asked. Exchanges of information can take place in a workroom or on a bus, but conversations that involve the heart need some planning to take place as people may need privacy to respond honestly. Dropping a bombshell in public isn't fair.

8

Respond to criticism with genuine humility.

When we're told that we've done/said something wrong, we can choose how we respond. We can reject the criticism, come back with our own, or we can accept it and hope to learn from it. Many times there is at least a grain of truth in the criticism, so we can make changes and be better people.

9

Examine body language for *real* meaning.

Our bodies often inadvertently reveal the meanings behind our words. Assessing our own body language, as well as that of the person we're speaking to, can help us discover a potential disconnect between words and true feelings. This can be addressed: "It doesn't seem like you're really ok with this solution by the way your arms are crossed."

10

Ask clarifying questions for better understanding.

Guessing games can be fun at a carnival, but they're dangerous in communication. Paraphrasing and asking clarifying questions is far preferable. "Do you want this assignment done by the end of the day today?" "Are you upset because I forgot or because I was with friends?" Have the right conversation by asking the right questions.

11

Substitute *and* for *but* in conversations.

Holding equal sentiments in tension is important to keeping communication flowing. Replacing "but" with the word "and" can help another person hear your true meaning. "I am angry at you, but I love you" might imply that the love is compromised by the anger. "I am angry at you *and* I love you" invites both parties to contribute to the conversation.

12

Feel free to complain; don't criticize.

The difference between complaint and criticism may be the difference between the success and failure of a relationship. Complaining focuses on an action or behavior you would like to see changed; criticism chips away at a person's value. It's the difference between, *That* was stupid and *You* are stupid.

13

Be patient; toxic communication heals slowly.

My husband once told me, when I asked if my hurtful conversation habits were improving, that it's like asking if stabbing someone five times a day is better than being stabbed twenty times a day. He was still bleeding and recovering from the damage I had inflicted. Changing patterns takes time, and so does healing. Be patient.

14

Communication denial: NOT knowing can hurt.

"What are you pretending not to know?" This is a question Susan Scott asks CEOs in her book *Fierce Conversations*. There is often an underlying knowing about what difficult conversation or action has to happen, but we avoid it by pretending it doesn't exist. That rarely helps! Have the hard conversation so things can move forward!

15

You can have confrontation without conflict.

Confrontation is not necessarily the same as conflict. Confrontation may simply be a face-to-face meeting. If we present the information clearly and without animosity, and if another person responds well, there may be no conflict. When two sides have opposing opinions or goals, a dispute may ensue. Even then, remembering the goal of the conversation will help cooler heads prevail.

16

Persuade or illustrate points with stories.

Anecdotes drive home a point unlike any other method of communication by connecting emotions to logic. Personal stories – whether they're ours or someone else's – can emphasize a point or make new information accessible, especially stories with strong emotions or well-placed humor. Stories are also less threatening when conversations may be sensitive.

17

Great power in *please* and *thanks*

Especially in our most intimate relationships, where familiarity often breeds contempt, using common courtesies reminds us of the value we place on people and our connection to them. Omitting words like *please* and *thank you* may communicate that we take an important person for granted or that we have less respect than we do. Manners matter!

18

Only improve, control one person: you.

We may want to speak into someone's life to make him easier to live with, but the only person's life we really can control is in the mirror. Our fervent desire to make someone else a good listener doesn't remove our need to practice those skills ourselves. The good news is that when we change, the dynamic has to change.

19

Being right doesn't win you friends.

Making sure that others know you're right doesn't help foster relationship or communication. Unless someone's life is at risk or there are dire consequences to a choice being made, we can keep our smug, correct facts to ourselves. You can keep score or you can be happy; it's hard to do both.

20

Avoid, *Everyone else agrees with me.*

It's rarely helpful to come to a conversation prepared to speak for anyone but yourself. When we use phrases like, *Everyone else agrees with me,* we either create group agreement that's not there to falsely boost our claim or we reveal that we've been gossiping behind someone's back. Neither scenario makes us look very good.

21

Use filter between thoughts and words.

As human beings, we are unique in the animal kingdom in that we have sufficient time between stimulus and response to formulate wise words and actions. We aren't obligated to respond with the first words that pop into our heads, and we aren't slaves to the emotions that may come to us unbidden. Breathe. Take. Time. To. Think. Before. Speaking.

Killing Me Softly: Wrecking Good Communication

22

Sarcasm often shuts down effective communication.

Some people feel that sarcasm is a particularly witty form of humor. For the most part, it runs a great risk of being misunderstood or hurtful, so it should be used sparingly and only in familiar settings. Since there's often a caustic edge to sarcasm, it can put a relational wedge between people, increasing mistrust and confusion.

23

Silent treatment communicates...not good things!

There's a profound difference between holding your tongue because you have nothing edifying to say and not speaking to someone to send a message that you're upset. If you think you're keeping silent because you can't trust yourself to speak, you may practice expressing words to that effect. "I don't want to discuss this right now because I'm still processing."

24

Avoid manipulation; it doesn't work out.

It may seem patently obvious to state that we shouldn't manipulate others, but behavior won't change until we recognize our errors. Manipulation has more to do with motives than words. What are we hoping for when we say things? Do we want things to go our way at any cost? Do we care about others? Using others is bad communication.

25

Incessant bragging...Don't be that guy!

Conversation is like tennis with equally matched players engaged on either side. The goals of communication are understanding and influence. Bragging about yourself undermines those goals and doesn't invite the other person to engage; he has to top your story or just listen. Be proud of accomplishments, but don't focus exclusively on them or you won't create common ground to build relationship.

26

Stop lying; it erodes relationship foundations.

The times in my life I've had my heart broken were because of lies. Once a lie is discovered, it takes time and great effort to rebuild the trust that's been lost. Honesty truly is the best policy; it eliminates the need to remember lies and it allows us to live with a clear conscience.

27

Gossip, slander undermine trust, spread lies.

Speaking poorly of others or spreading stories (true or not) reveals more about you than it does about them. Ask, "Why do I feel compelled to share this information?" If it's truly to inform so action can be taken, share wisely. If it's to make someone look bad or to manipulate, bite your tongue.

28

Name calling is childish, causes defensiveness.

If you've witnessed name calling on a children's playground, you know the colorful and creative names that youngsters can hurl in the heat of a moment. Adults don't always grow out of that, but it halts any hope of future conversation and understanding as the wounded party has to recover some dignity. Name calling is childish; we're adults.

29

Triangulation causes communication strangulation, so don't!

Triangulation is simply talking to any person other than the person you should be talking to, creating a "triangle" of communication that disallows any effective action from taking place. If Jack isn't doing his job right, don't tell Angie; tell Jack so he can get the help he needs and keep the respect he deserves.

30

Avoid extreme language like *always, never.*

Extreme language like *always* and *never* often stems from intense emotions or lack of understanding. Whether it's an author's careless statement that *everyone* has experienced such-and-such or a spouse spewing angry words of frustration, broad generalizations are rarely effective. Response? "Not always!" "Not everyone!" We get distracted by the minutiae and exceptions.

31

One-word answers don't move conversations.

When I was young, my mom encouraged me to answer adults' questions with more than simply yes or no. When we use one-word answers the conversation becomes an interview instead of the desired give and take of true communication. Answer interestingly and then ask a related question in return. Conversation takes two people or it's a monologue!

32

H.A.L.T – don't have crucial conversations now!

The acronym H.A.L.T. stands for *Hungry, Angry, Lonely, Tired* and refers to conditions that should preclude us from having crucial conversations or making monumental decisions. When we are emotionally or physically compromised, we aren't in control of our words. Practice saying, "I want to talk about this, but now is not a good time." You'll be glad you did.

33

It's not me, is it? Defensiveness

A focus on defending ourselves in conversation may indicate profound insecurity or a fixed mindset that needs to constantly prove one's worth. The alternative is to invite feedback – even criticism – with a desire to learn and grow in the future from mistakes made. Own your mistakes and learn from them. Accountability is a good quality.

34

Hyperbole is the worst thing EVER!

Hyperbole, or exaggeration, impedes effective communication. Remember the story of the boy who cried wolf? After alerting the village many times that there was a wolf when there wasn't, nobody believed him when there was real danger. Hyperbolic language undermines credibility, so only say the food was amazing when it really was better than anything you've had.

35

Accusations: pointing fingers without hearing truth

J'accuse! Accusations based on fact and requiring action to obtain justice are far different than refusing to hear facts and throwing a colleague or loved one under the bus to save your reputation or express anger or hurt feelings. Be sure to hear all sides of a story before blaming another and questioning motives. You might save face, too.

36

Condescension is demeaning and causes anger.

Belittling someone to make yourself feel more important is the antithesis of effective communication. Condescension is closely linked to arrogance, and it repels others instead of inviting them to engage, thereby undermining the goals of communication: understanding and influence. If you can't refrain simply because it's mean, do it to improve your chances of being heard.

Communicating Professionally: Making Good Impressions Last

37

Written communication reflects you, your business.

Written communication like marketing materials, online content, business cards, and emails, is a reflection of you and your business. If you're accurate and responsive in written communication, colleagues and potential clients will believe that you run a quality operation. In people's minds, careless writing may equate to careless business.

38

Yes, spelling counts. So does punctuation!

Students often asks their teachers, "Does spelling count?" What difference does it make?! If not, will you spell phonetically? If so, will you try harder? Spelling, grammar, and punctuation count in school and in business. Be intentional with your words so that you are perceived as educated and articulate. Proofread and spell check – they will save your bacon!

39

Ending emails with thank you: careful!

Many emails end with the words thank you as a courtesy. This pair of words is often followed by a comma and the sender's name, and the structure is common and accepted, but grammatically incorrect. Its effect is to thank yourself as the sender. More appropriate signature words would describe the intent or emotions of the sender. *Warmly... Sincerely... Regards...*

40

Know which communication method is best.

Do you require a quick response to a question of information? A text might be appropriate. Afraid words or intentions might be misinterpreted? Better stick with a phone call or face-to-face meeting. Facts that need to be documented with action items? Email will do the job. Consider audience, time frame, and information needed.

41

Reserve salty for cooking, not language!

Mature adults know that different audiences and contexts call for a variety of communication. Sunday afternoon watching sports is perfectly appropriate for expletives and colorful adjectives; a business environment is not. Even at networking events that may include alcohol or entertainment, one should be wary of using double entendres or offensive language.

42

Firm handshakes show confidence and stability.

Because there's no way to know if a new acquaintance will have a monumental impact on our lives, it's important to make a good first impression, starting with confident handshake. A firm grasp at the juncture of the thumb and forefinger, with two or three solid pumps says, "I mean business, but I'm not trying to control you."

43

Smile when introducing yourself to others.

Smiles are contagious and good for us! A smile changes our brain chemistry by releasing endorphins to help manage stress and has a positive effect on us and on those around us. It communicates confidence and a pleasant disposition, which are both qualities that attract others to us professionally and personally. Let a smile be part of a first impression!

44

Have and maintain a positive outlook.

It's been said that success is going from failure to failure without losing enthusiasm. This isn't to say that we accept defeat unquestioningly, but that we learn with our chins up and move forward. Every group benefits from at least a subtle cheerleader to encourage when the going gets tough. "Yes, we can!" versus "What's the point?"

45

Tell brief, interesting anecdotes in conversation.

One of the most effective ways to illustrate points or persuade listeners is through stories. While facts may be convincing, stories tap into common human experiences in ways that can galvanize and unite groups for a cause. Even in more intimate settings, stories can put people at ease, which makes you seem like a pretty great person to be around!

46

Be inclusive of everyone in groups.

Networking and group settings like conferences can make us feel awkward and diffident so we don't always think of others. Whether we're at a business luncheon or an after-hours Chamber of Commerce event, we will make a good impression if we remember to ask questions of and include everyone in group conversations. Be aware of body language, too.

47

Ask interesting questions to facilitate conversation.

If you've attended a networking event and someone has asked, "What business are you in?" you know that there could be more interesting ways to start conversations. Think of creative ways to engage: "What's your favorite part of your job?" "What have you learned about yourself in this business?" Interesting questions elicit more interesting communication.

48

Find topics common to all participants.

It's a relief to meet someone in a professional setting and immediately have something in common. Both Cubs fans? What are the chances! Have a place on Maui? Me, too! But people can very quickly feel left out of the conversation if the topic isn't relevant. Current events (carefully!), weather, business climate, etc. are better topics than niche interests.

49

Flattery/criticism "sandwich" is rarely effective.

You may have heard, "You're a great employee, but you've lost so many clients. At least you dress nicely!" It's meant to soften the blow of challenging feedback, but it's manipulative and makes people suspicious. Try, "You're better at X than Y, so do more X." Or just shoot straight and be brief. Nobody's fooled by the flattering lead-in.

50

Be **A**udible, **B**old, **C**oncise in presentations.

Not everyone is a professional speaker, but almost everyone has to give announcements or presentations from time to time. Here are ABCs to help make this process less stressful. Be **A**udible so everyone can hear you. Use a microphone. Be **B**old and say what you mean without apology. Get in; get out. Practice so you can be **C**oncise and effective.

51

Utilize repetition, utilize repetition, utilize repetition.

Restate points that seem to be misunderstood the first time, and repeat verbatim points that need to be emphasized. There are procedures that must be followed exactly. There is a mission statement that frames everything about the company. Since this information is crucial, it behooves us to introduce it from different angles in different contexts to keep it fresh.

52

Only use examples illustrating main point.

When giving a presentation, know what your main point is and make sure everything else relates to or supports that point. If it doesn't, take it out. Save it for another talk. This eliminates the rambling, nonsensical monologues people hear when speakers don't stick to the point. Stories are effective to make a point, but have a point to make!

Word Usage: Say What You Mean

53

You're in *your* car; that's right.

Your indicates possession: Where are *your* pants? *You're* is a contraction of *you* and *are*. If the word could be replaced with those two words, then you need an apostrophe. *You're* a knucklehead. *You're* welcome. (Yes. That's how you spell that.) If nothing else, remember this equation: *you* + *are* = *you're*.

54

Their, they're, there: trifecta of turmoil

Their denotes possession: I'm borrowing *their* car. Remove the first letter, you have the word *heir*, a person who inherits money. *There* indicates a location: *There* are so many ants! If you remove the first letter, you have *here*. *Here* is a location, too. *They're* combines *they* and *are*. *They're* coming over at midnight. *They're* over *there* with *their* coffee.

55

Two, to, too: trouble in triplicate

These homonyms cause trouble wherever they go. Let's start with a sentence using all three to demonstrate the difference.

I'll add *two* sugars *to* my coffee, *too*.

Two is a number. *To* is a preposition (like over, above, around) that indicates direction. And if something is in addition, you use *too*; it has an additional *o*.

56

Things aren't *kind of,* *very unique.*

Unique means *being the only one of its kind.* There is only one. Like a snowflake. It's an extreme word that needs no modifier. Therefore, things and people aren't *rather* or *very* unique. They are unique or something else. When at a loss, descriptions like *special, unusual,* or *unfamiliar* may be more appropriate and should be used.

57

Than versus *then*: comparison or time

These two words don't actually sound alike. And they certainly don't mean the same thing. *Than* indicates comparison: Jack is smarter *than* Hank. *Then* indicates events sequential in time: I ate the cheese, *then* I drank the wine. *Then* contains *hen*. Which came first: chicken (hen) or egg? It's a question of time. Use *then*.

58

Supposedly is the word; not supposably.

We use the word *supposedly* to describe actions that are based on an assumption of certain facts being true. It can imply, however, that there is some doubt.

You say you went to the store, but your track record and length of time you were gone makes me wonder.

And the word is not supposably.

59

Expand vocabulary and use words correctly.

The only thing worse than using boring vocabulary is using colorful words incorrectly. I once heard someone use *motif* instead of *coif* to describe a client's hair. Oops. It's noble and effective communication to learn new words; just be sure to actually learn them. Look them up. Use them in sentences to test the waters.

60

Irony isn't the same as coincidence.

When someone mentions a show that you just watched, that's coincidence, not irony. When Alanis Morissette croons about a traffic jam when you're already late, she's describing unfortunate situations, but they aren't ironic. Taking a specific route in traffic when you're running late because it's known to be a short cut is ironic if that route made you even later.

61

He is *good*; he does *well*.

You may remember your high school English teacher telling you that adjectives modify nouns and adverbs modify verbs. That's the difference between *good* and *well*. *Good* is an adjective, used to describe nouns: This soup is *good*. High quality, *good* flavor, nice consistency. *Well* is an adverb used to describe verbs: She dances *well*. How? *Well*.

72

62

Don't *literally* laugh your head off.

Figurative language uses words in a way to make a point in communication or literature. They are often expressions using metaphors or similes: *Looking at this fire is like looking into the sun!* Literal language means exactly what it says: I *literally* just arrived. People don't *literally* cry their eyes out. Nor do things *literally* make heads explode. Not possible.

63

Lay something down; *lie* down yourself.

The official explanation of the difference between *lie* and *lay* is that *lay* takes a direct object and *lie* does not. Why don't you *lie* down for a while? *Lay* the book on the table. Point of confusion: when using them in the past tense, *lay* becomes *laid* and *lie* becomes *lay*.

64

Waiters wait on tables, not friends.

There are often geographic areas within the same country where expressions evolve, even when incorrect. If you are from the southeastern United States, you may think that anybody can wait on people, whereas other parts of the country know that only servers in restaurants do that. We wait *for* a bus; we wait *in* line; servers wait *on* restaurant patrons.

65

Movies *affect* me; they have *effects*.

The word *affect* is a verb; *effect* is a noun. One way to remember the difference is that *affect* describes an action, and they both begin with *a*. An action or system is *effective* because it has positive *effects*. The exception is when someone has a demeanor or emotion that seems unnatural for the situation at hand.

66

Morphine's a *drug*; not past *drag*.

Some irregular verbs in English are so problematic that incorrect forms become commonplace. The past tense of the verb to *drag* fits that category. I *drag*, I *dragged*. The word *drug* is only used to refer to pharmaceuticals or illegal substances. The burglar will *drug* the homeowner; he *drugged* him.

67

Precise language, please. *Exactly* right words.

Effective written and oral communication is based on precision of language. It makes our writing more interesting and it conveys more of our exact feelings and meanings. Try saying exactly what you mean. You're not really, really tired; you're *exhausted* or *weary*. Instead of being mad, try being *incensed* or *infuriated*. Or are you more *frustrated*? *Indignant*?

68

Quote/Unquote goes before/after quote.

Whether in writing or with our fingers in conversation, quotation marks are often misplaced and overused. When speaking, say, *"Quote, cleanliness is next to godliness, unquote."* When writing, place the first set of quotation marks at the beginning of the direct quote and the second set afterwards, enclosing punctuation inside. *"Speak only if it improves upon the silence."* ~ Gandhi

69

Give reports to Jane or *myself.*

You may have heard this in a meeting, but it's incorrect. The only time I can use *myself* in a sentence is when *I* am the subject. *I* can see *myself*. The correct version of that sentence is: Give the report to Jane or *me.* Try removing the other person's name: *You can give the report to myself.* Awkward...

70

It's versus *Its*: contraction or possession

This is among the most common mistakes that I've encountered. Apostrophes are only used for contraction or possession, so if the word can be replaced with "it is," then use an apostrophe; *it's* a contraction. If not – if referring to an object already mentioned - use *its*. The refrigerator is on *its* last legs; *it's* going to die soon.

71

Quotation marks are just for quotes.

Quotation marks around a word do not provide emphasis in a sentence. Their intended purpose is to directly quote what's been said. Therefore, reading that employees must "wash" hands after using the restroom raises suspicions about the cleanliness of the organization. "Delicious" baked goods are also dubious. Misused quotation marks serve to convey sarcasm. Wink, wink....

72

Oxford comma creates clarity, eliminates confusion.

The Oxford comma, named after the Oxford Press, which favors it, is the comma after the penultimate item in a list. Without it there may be confusion: *I'd like to thank my parents, Ayn Rand and God.* Wait. Are Ayn and God your parents? Behold clarity in punctuation: *I'd like to thank my parents, Ayn Rand, and God.*

73

Who is subject; *whom* is object.

Subjects act; objects receive action. If the person acting or being acted upon is unknown, *who* or *whom* are appropriate pronouns. But which is which? *Who* is a subject and does the action of a sentence; *whom* receives action. *Who* likes ice cream? I like ice cream! With *whom* did you speak? I spoke with Dan.

74

She and I?
Her and me?

This example has an added dimension of speakers wanting to sound educated and proper when they are actually saying something wrong. Favorite Facebook example? Here's a picture of *Sophie and I.* Remove Sophie's name and you'll see the error: Here's a picture of *I?* Not so much. *She and I* went.... You came with *her and me.* Those are right.

75

Drink *less* milk, eat *fewer* beans.

If you can count things, you have more or *fewer* of them. I ate *more* protein bars. I ate *fewer* protein bars.

If you can't count something, use *less*. I drank *more* beer. I drank *less* beer.

There aren't *less* students; there are *fewer* students. You can count them. Now you can make *fewer* errors in this area. You're welcome.

76

Apostrophes never, ever make anything plural.

This shouldn't need any further explanation, but indulge me. When something happens every week on the same day, that event occurs on *Wednesdays*. There is no need to add an apostrophe. Even if you have several televisions, you have TVs. No apostrophe. This holiday card is from the *Smiths*. NO APOSTROPHE!

77

Use commas when directly addressing someone.

A direct address comma is used to set off a person's name when you are speaking to him, whether you use his name first or at the end of the sentence. The rule applies to nicknames, as well.

Hello, Mary. Jake, are you coming over?

Did you eat, Terry? (Without a comma: *Did you eat Terry?* No!)

You go, girl!

78

Dangling modifiers are awkward and confusing.

Modifiers are used to describe. It might be an adjective or a whole clause modifying a noun and should be placed as close as possible to that which they describe.

Leaking, my brother brought up a bottle of cider. Clearly my brother was not leaking in the cellar. So...

My brother brought up a bottle of cider that was leaking.

79

Semicolons separate sentences; no comma splices!

Semicolons, underused and misunderstood, separate two complete sentences that could stand alone, separated by a period, but are so closely related that a more intimate grammatical relationship is appropriate. Comma splices are caused when a comma is used instead of a semicolon or period. *The sentences after semicolons begin with lower case letters; a capital isn't necessary.*

80

The difference between singular, plural possessives

Although apostrophes are tiny, they can wreak communication havoc. Therefore, they warrant more than one lesson. When one item belongs to one person, add apostrophe + s: This is the *boy's* book.

When an item belongs to several people, add s + apostrophe: These are the *boys'* books.

Children, men, and women are already plural. These are *women's* clothes.

81

If only you were using subjunctive...

The *subjunctive* is used to describe wishes and subjective circumstances and in certain fixed expressions. The *indicative* is used to express facts.

Subjunctive examples: *If I were king..., Is it necessary that we be here? He demanded that she leave.*

Indicative example: Almost every other sentence we use. ☺

82

Who's going? Jake, *whose* car exploded.

Again with the apostrophes! Yes. *Who's* is a contraction of *who is*, so if the word you're searching for could be replaced with those two words, use *who's*. If, on the other hand, the word you want indicates ownership, you want to use *whose*.

Who's coming with me? *(Who is...)*

Is this the girl *whose* mom yelled at us?

83

The thought trails off. . . Use ellipses.

An ellipsis is the dot, dot, dot (three) indicating that words have been left out of a quote or that a thought trails off and the reader is left to imagine the outcome.

If only I had . . . well, it doesn't matter now.

Caveat: When omitting words in a quote, don't change the meaning of the sentence!

When Things Get Heated: Cooling Communication

84

Gratitude and curiosity bring collaborative solutions.

Empathy and gratitude can turn around a confrontation.

You forgot milk. Crazy day? vs *You forgot milk. You're so unreliable.*

Thanking another for efforts and asking for explanations allows us to collaborate on a solution instead of focusing on whose fault it is.

85

Take a break from heated conversations.

When heart rates rise, research indicates that decisions aren't clear and communication suffers. This is when we regret words we speak in anger. It's often wise to pause robust dialogues until emotional equilibrium can be reached. But when taking a break, be clear that you will come back to continue the conversation and determine a time to do so.

86

Stories in our heads aren't facts.

Stating facts instead of starting with the story you've made up in your head ensures that everyone is hearing the same story, as far as it is possible. Stating facts is less threatening and there is less need to become defensive. Stating facts doesn't give room for argument because the facts are objective. How we interpret the facts may vary, but we can start with the same information.

87

Apologies: own up when you're wrong.

It is difficult to overestimate the impact of a well-placed, heartfelt, articulate apology, especially if you can apologize before the other person comes to you to tell you what you did wrong. If you know you've erred or hurt another's feelings, run – don't walk – to say, "I'm sorry I did/said. . ." Be specific and sincere; then move on.

88

Power of forgiveness – giving and asking

The final piece of an apology is the restorative act of asking for forgiveness. This allows the other person to close the loop or express further grievances to clear the air. Without it, resentment or unspoken issues may linger. When wronged, we extend forgiveness for our own benefit; holding a grudge only hurts us.

89

"Please tell me more about that."

This phrase is useful when someone is accusing you or explaining reasons for being hurt. Defensiveness is the natural reaction, but asking for more feedback instead will open dialogue and diffuse emotional tension. It can also be useful to elicit crucial information for a decision or action that needs to be taken. It implies a true desire to understand.

Honor and Respect: Living It Out

90

Assume the best: benefit of doubt

I didn't drive well the day my 8-year-old was diagnosed with cancer, so I can give others the benefit of the doubt when they drive poorly, too. Why not extend the principle to other situations? Maybe my boss didn't intend to slight me; perhaps I'm genuinely less qualified. Receive a terse email? Maybe the sender was short on time, not angry.

91

Give others time to process change.

Leaders and parents often have information about forthcoming change. When we communicate the information, we may get pushback, emotion, and/or resistance. When possible, give others time to adjust to information you've already processed so they, too, can make decisions and respond appropriately. "I know this is new information, so let's talk later if you have questions."

92

Use words of affirmation to encourage.

Conversations that include correction can be made much easier if we pave the way with succinct, specific words of encouragement when others excel. No need to "butter up" with flattery before dropping the hammer if others have been affirmed in areas of strength and accomplishment at regular intervals. When someone struggles, positive words can also help build relationship.

93

Don't interrupt others when they speak.

If you come from a large family, interrupting is necessary to be heard, but in small groups or one-on-one, letting someone finish a complete thought is a way to confer dignity and move conversation forward. Interrupting while another is speaking says, "My thoughts are more important than what you have to say." Patience brings understanding and respect.

94

Make eye contact when in conversation.

Looking someone in the eye when shaking hands and meeting for the first time conveys confidence. Eye contact during significant dialogue communicates that you are fully present and engaged in the conversation. Checking phones or looking over someone's shoulders while she's talking says, "Is there someone more important I should be talking to?" People deserve our undivided attention.

95

Shine the light on someone else.

People remember how we make them feel more than what we say. Therefore, when we give others credit for their ideas and allow them to flourish, we make them feel valued and accomplished. Conversely, insisting that we get recognition at someone else's expense or hogging the limelight will make them feel slighted and insignificant. It's not always about you!

96

You can be kind AND candid.

It's possible, and, in fact, more kind! Stating the facts without maligning someone's character allows everyone to learn from mistakes. If I broke the system, I need to know or I'll do it again! When we're trying to spare someone's feelings, we actually allow more frustration than if we simply had the right conversation in the first place.

97

Companionable silence: supporting someone without speaking

A novel I once read referred to people sitting in "companionable silence." Job's friends sat with him without speaking. Simply being with someone when she is struggling, sad, or grieving is a powerful way to communicate support. It's the good kind of "silent treatment," allowing another to feel your presence without feeling judgment or hearing advice.

98

Do what you say you'll do.

Whether it's with a client or a loved one, the most successful and cost-effective way to demonstrate integrity, build trust in a new relationship, or rebuild trust when it's been broken is to let your "yes" be "yes" and your "no" be "no." Follow up on emails. Respond to phone calls. Keep promises.

99

Catch people doing well; praise them.

The best surprise is a good surprise, so when children or coworkers are doing what they're supposed to be doing, but they're doing it exceptionally, depositing a well-timed, "Way to rock that phone call!" connects us in positive ways to others. Often called a "hit and run compliment," it's disarming and encouraging.

100

Genuinely encourage others to give opinions.

Nobody wins when only the boss or the parent can have good ideas or get credit for them. Not every decision calls for collaboration of ideas and opinions, but when someone is skilled in a particular area, why not let him give opinions? This keeps leadership accessible and creativity flowing for better results. Nobody wants sycophants agreeing to bad ideas.

Conclusion

It's nearly impossible to practice flawless communication skills in every conversation, but employing even just a few of these lessons at a time may make it easier to avoid mangled exchanges and to engage effectively with those around you. Susan Scott said in her book *Fierce Conversations,* "Speak and listen as if this is the most important conversation you will ever have with this person. It could be. Participate as if it matters. It does." Whether your stumbling block is grammar or responding to criticism, these tools can help you move forward to understand and influence those around you to make the world you live in a better place.

About the *Six-Word Lessons Series*

Legend has it that Ernest Hemingway was challenged to write a story using only six words. He responded with the story, "For sale: baby shoes, never worn." The story tickles the imagination. Why were the shoes never worn? The answers are left up to the reader's imagination.

This style of writing has a number of aliases: postcard fiction, flash fiction, and micro fiction. Lonnie Pacelli was introduced to this concept in 2009 by a friend, and started thinking about how this extreme brevity could apply to today's communication culture of text messages, tweets and Facebook posts. He wrote the first book, *Six-Word Lessons for Project Managers*, then started helping other authors write and publish their own books in the series.

The books all have six-word chapters with six-word lesson titles, each followed by a one-page description. They can be written by entrepreneurs who want to promote their businesses, or anyone with a message to share.

See the entire *Six-Word Lessons Series* at 6wordlessons.com

45991464R00066